Copyright

Title book: My First Book about Animals in the World
Author book: Jessica L. Williams

© 2021, Jessica L. Williams
Self publishing
Jlw7462894@yahoo.com

DEDICATED TO ALL

ANIMAL LOVERS

MY FIRST BOOK
ABOUT
ANIMALS
IN THE WORLD

CAT

TIGER

FOX

LION

DOG

PANDA

BABOON

BEAR

KOALA

GORILLA

PARROT

OWL

FLAMINGO

BIRD

OSTRICH

PELICAN

GIRAFFE

DONKEY

HORSE

SHEEP

ZEBRA

COW

PIG

KANGAROO

GOAT

ELEPHANT

CHAMELEON

SNAKE

HAMSTER

SQUIRREL

DEER

RABBIT

PORCUPINE

ROOSTER

RAT

PENGUIN

DUCK

TURTLE

OPOSSUM

PEACOCK

ALLIGATOR

FROG

THIS IS THE END.
SAY GOODBYE TO ALL YOUR ANIMAL FRIENDS!